Henry Taunt
of Oxford

Henry Taunt
of Oxford

A Victorian Photographer

Malcolm Graham

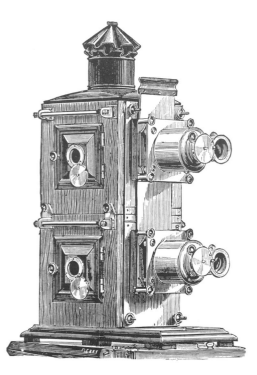

 1973
The Oxford Illustrated Press

AUTHOR'S NOTE

I should like to thank all those people who have helped make this book a reality. They include not only my informants, without whom the book would have been much thinner, but also J. P. Wells, the Oxford City Librarian, who has given me the benefit of his advice and encouragement.

In particular, I should like to pay tribute to the work of Bryan Brown and the late Mary Nichols, who began the task of rescuing Taunt's life from unjustified obscurity.

This book is published in co-operation with the City of Oxford Library Committee, and royalties from its sale will be devoted to the improvement of the Local History Collection.

Film prepared by Oxford Litho Plates, Oxford

Printed by Blackwells, Oxford

ISBN 0 902280 14 7

The Oxford Illustrated Press
Shelley Close, Kiln Lane,
Risinghurst, Oxford

© 1973 The Oxford Illustrated Press and the author

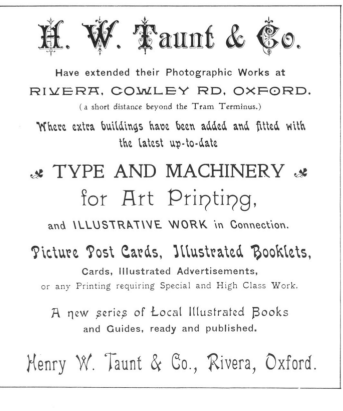

Contents

＊ TO ALL OUR FRIENDS. ＊

———

A greeting to you, worthy friend,
   May you enjoy our pages here ;
If error you should find, please send
   And tell us how to make it clear.
We've done our best your wants to fill,
   To put down all just so and so,
But errors may have crept in still,
   And if they have, please let us know.

" All photographs have some limited historical value; those taken today will many of them be much wanted in fifty years' time."

H. W. Taunt, 1918

1 Penson's Gardens, 1912. The boys are standing outside the house where Taunt was born.

1. TAUNT'S EARLY LIFE

Many an incident did we meet with and many a small adventure, trifling in themselves but each representing something that added to the tendency of the way we should afterwards go.

H. W. Taunt, June 1913

During an evening thunderstorm on 14 June 1842, and while Great Tom was sounding the Curfew, Henry William Taunt was born in Oxford at Pensons Gardens, St. Ebbe's.[1] It was a fitting start to the life of a remarkable Oxonian, who, though largely self-taught, became well-known as a photographer and author, as a publisher and entertainer, and, not least, as a memorable local character.

Taunt was the son of ' poor but respectable and respected parents ', his father, Henry, being a Bletchingdon-born plumber and glazier, and his mother, Martha, a country girl from the Berkshire village of West Ilsley. They could not afford to give him a good, formal education, but probably sent him to the church school in St. Ebbe's whenever possible. In later life, he also recalled spending an enjoyable time at West Ilsley school while holidaying there with his grandparents.

From the first, Taunt showed a great interest in his surroundings, and must indeed have been something of a truant. He frequently sailed down Trill Mill Stream in summer to avoid paying 6d. at Folly Bridge lock, and on one occasion fell into the stream, receiving a good hiding when he returned home soaking wet. He was not to be put off by punishments or warnings, however, and, against his parents' wishes, he played with the sons of a drunken old bricklayer, Timmy Bricknell, because ' these boys were older than ourselves and cunning street Arabs with no end of tricks'.

But if these were exploits common to boys in all ages, Taunt's memory and powers of observation were far more

2 The inner Gate of the Franciscan Friary, *c.* 1848.

3 26 High Street being demolished for the new front of Brasenose College, 1887.

unusual. When he prepared his folder on the Greyfriars district of St. Ebbe's in 1912, for example, he included a sketch of the inner gate of the Franciscan Friary in Charles Street, which had been pulled down when he was about 8 years old.[2] He also noted that Turnagain Lane was the original name for Charles Street, because wheeled traffic had to turn back to Littlegate Street when it reached the Friars' gateway. These childhood recollections show at an early stage the 'keen observation' and 'tenacious memory' which were to make Taunt an outstanding photographer.

A career in photography was still remote, however, and 'in those days, boys had to begin work when young to help fill the cupboard at home'. At first, he worked with his father, but he was against the idea of becoming a plumber, and, in about 1853, he joined Embling the tailor at 23 High Street, earning 4/– a week, and reading or painting in the back of the shop during quiet afternoons. His next job, with a stationer called Ladd, was 'too hard', and he found a more congenial atmosphere at the High Street bookshop and auction room of Charles Richards. Despite having to work from 7 a.m. to 9 p.m. for only 5/– or 5/6 a week, Taunt stayed there for two years, enjoying the job and gaining respect for Richards' honesty.

Away from work, Taunt's physical and intellectual horizons were gradually widening. At the age of 13, he went to an ox-roast on the frozen Thames at Kennington, and, in the following year, he and a companion went bird-shooting on Cumnor Hill. He also paid a visit to Kirtlington, and saw someone put in the stocks, noting that 'so much sympathy was expressed and so many mugs of beer were offered and drank from, that the last state of the man . . . was worse than when he was first [put] there'. In themselves, these were small adventures, but they may have stimulated Taunt's interest in photography, and encouraged him to improve his knowledge. This he did by reading a good many books in Richards' shop during 'the vacation when things were very leisurely', and by going to Crake's School in Clifton Hampden for part of 1859 'to get some education'.

2. HIS CAREER

Your own works—so many—are a memorial to and of yourself which will stand forever.
            D. P. Watkins, Manager of the Church Army Press,
                                             August 1910

The decisive step in Taunt's life came in 1856 when he left Richards to join the staff of Edward Bracher, who was the pioneer of photography in Oxford, and who then had a shop at 26 High Street.[3] For some years, Bracher had enjoyed a prosperous monopoly in the city, and, although 'none of the rooms were large enough to swing round the proverbial cat . . . Dons and Laity and Ladies and Gentlemen of every class all made their way up those squeaking stairs' to be photographed. Taunt began as a general utility hand, but, after a German called Werner had been dismissed he was given the outdoor work, and photographed his first Oxford crew in Exeter College quad in about 1858.

Business interests, increasing competition and decreasing profit margins forced Bracher to sell his business to Wheeler and Day in 1863, but Taunt stayed on as photographic manager. By this time, Taunt was well-established as a photographer, and his early concentration upon portrait work—then the more lucrative side of the business—was being supplemented by 'a pronounced inclination for architecture and landscape'. This new phase was probably a straightforward development of his boyhood interests, but it may also have stemmed from a solitary, and dangerous, trip which he made up the Thames from Oxford to Lechlade and back during Christmas 1859. Despite a near disaster at Hart's Weir on his return journey, Taunt's love of the Thames was confirmed, and he remembered the expedition fifty years later as vividly as if it had just occurred. The varied scenery, the people he met and the things he saw persuaded him that the river had been unduly neglected not only as a subject for the camera but also as a place of recreation. He set out to rectify both these omissions soon afterwards, and his earliest photographs of the Thames date from 1860 and 1861.

Taunt's ambitions, and the ready market for photographs which existed in Oxford, encouraged him to set up his own business as soon as he could. By 1866, he was living at 67 George Street, but he does not seem to have left Wheeler and Day's until two years later. As soon as this connection was broken, he opened a shop in St. John's—now St. Bernard's—Road, but soon found it more convenient to operate from premises at his own home in George Street.

Taunt proved to be a highly astute businessman, keeping standards high and costs low, while seeking publicity whenever possible. In January 1869, it was announced that Taunt had published a Shilling Series of photographic views—an extensive collection, covering Oxford and neighbourhood. A reviewer wrote that 'no expense appears to have been spared to obtain the finest result possible', and yet the photographs 'are . . . published at a price which places them within reach of every class of the community'. In July, the *Wiltshire and Gloucestershire Standard,* having examined some of his new views, pronounced them to be 'amongst the best specimens of the photographic art that we have ever seen', and, no doubt at Taunt's prompting, emphasised the trouble he took over fixing and washing the prints 'the omission of which causes the picture to colour and fade'.

These views were so successful that Taunt was able to move to a more prominent shop at 33 Cornmarket Street during 1869,[4] and his flair for attracting publicity soon found new outlets. On 22 June 1870, for example, a correspondent of the *Standard* was 'attracted to a crowd opposite a photographer's shop in the Corn Market Street'. Scenting a story, he went nearer, and saw 'the object that the crowd has in view. It is a transparency of a most excellent photograph taken instantaneously by Mr Taunt of the procession of boats a few hours ago.' In the following year, Taunt began a new career as a lecturer, taking an audience of Oxford Churchmen on a trip down the Thames on 19 January 1871. Reports were again highly complimentary, and the *Oxford Times* could 'not but speak in terms of unqualified praise of the beauty of the views, which were of unusual excellence'.

4   33 Cornmarket Street, *c.* 1875.

5 Taunt and his assistants by the river, *c.* 1870.

By this time, Taunt's reputation was firmly established, and he became official photographer to the Oxford Architectural and Historical Society in 1871; far from resting upon his laurels, however, he determined to publish his work on the Thames in a book which would include a new survey, many photographs, and both historical and current information. The venture clearly involved a great deal of labour and expense, and, as he later pointed out, all his attempts to popularise the river ' were . . . carried out at our own cost, without the slightest help from the Commissioners or the Conservators of the river in any way whatever '. Nevertheless, he saved money by using a cleverly-designed boat which housed him, his two assistants and all their equipment during their summer expeditions on the river[5]. When *A New Map of the River Thames* appeared in 1872, it was an immediate success with artists, anglers, oarsmen and tourists, and the map, at a scale of 2 inches to 1 mile, probably led to Taunt's election as a Fellow of the Royal Geographical Society in 1893. Several subsequent editions of the book appeared, and Taunt's work was made known to a much larger public both in Britain and in the United States.

To pay for this book, and probably, one feels, because of his many interests, Taunt continued to diversify his business.

In 1871–72 he had a shop in Friar's Entry selling cheap window glass, and, in about 1875, he opened a new branch at 81 Easton Street, High Wycombe, which appears to have been run by Fanny Miles—later his housekeeper, and reputedly his mistress. During this period, he was also making lecture tours every winter, describing the Thames to large audiences, and receiving flattering reviews wherever he went. Only in Princes Risborough did he meet with apparent apathy—a sarcastic reporter attributing this 'to the apparent distaste existing in this place for anything scientific or artistic.'

The enthusiastic response to these lectures and his fondness for children persuaded Taunt to become an entertainer in a lighter vein. In February 1873, he began a long series of annual children's parties in the Town Hall, entertaining the children with comic songs, Magic Lantern readings and amusing plays—writing and arranging most of the material himself.[6] These parties always seem to have been popular, and not merely for their novelty. Of one in January 1874, the *Banbury Advertiser* wrote: ' the display was vastly superior to the usual class of these entertainments, and gave great satisfaction. Amongst the stories we may mention *Puss in Boots* and *Snow White,* both being well rendered, whilst the funny adventures of *Fritz and his Sledge* gave rise to roars of laughter, and caused a large fund of amusement.' The demand for these entertainments was clearly insatiable, and, by 1874, Taunt was offering ' Magic Lanterns or Dissolving View Apparatus, Screens, Slides, Gas Bags, Prepared Oil, Oxygen Gas, and every requisite for Magic Lantern Entertainments for Sale or Hire '.

PART III.
DAME WIGGINS OF LEE,
AND HER WONDERFUL CATS, THE FARMER, AND THE MAGICIENNE.
Written and Arranged Specially for this Entertainment by **MR. HENRY W. TAUNT.**

Dame Wiggins	... ... MISS LATISPER	Magicienne	... ... MISS MORETON
Farmer	... ... MR. BRENNER	Tommy	... ... MISS H. LATISPER
Jumbo	... ... MASTER G. LATISPER	Kitty	... ... MASTER H. LATISPER
Tiny	... ... MISS GRAY	Frisky	... ... MASTER BROOKE
Sandy	... ... MISS EDWARDS	Topsy	... ... MISS GORDON
Tabby	... ... MISS MOORE	Jenny	... ... MISS HOPE
Darky	... ... MISS PRICE	Brownie	... ... MASTER MELVILLE
Judy	... ... MASTER GILBERT	Daisy	... ... ,, ... MISS WEST

The Masks by **MR. J. WHITE,** Perruquier, Oxford.

The Dresses, &c., by **MRS.** and **MISS LATISPER** and **MRS. TAUNT.**

Lime Lights by **MR. TAUNT'S** Assistants. Bussonette and Bells, **MR. TAUNT.**

SYLLABUS.
Opening—The Cats indulge in a chorus, in the midst of which Dame Wiggins arrives—The Cats crowd round and welcome her—She expresses her gratification at coming home, and after praising them, sings them a song about her journey—The Cats then go to School, but two of them begin fighting about a stool, when the noise brings Dame Wiggins in, and she begins beating them, and compels them to behave—The Cats are then put through their examination, at which most of them fail, but finally Jumbo succeeds in answering, and the Dame is so pleased that she takes them off to play in the wood—Three of them cannot find their hats, and are left behind, they sing a trio, and at last, after a lot of hunting about, they find them, and leave to join the others—The Cats return from the wood, bringing a lost lamb, which they feed and put to bed, singing a lullaby, and soon after the Farmer comes, discovers the lamb, and wants to take it away, but the Cats resist, and force him out of the scene—Just at that moment the Magicienne appears, and, waving her wand, brings the Cats back—She then asks them to wish, and they reply by a Chorus—The Magicienne transforms the Cats into Children, and asks everyone to join in singing **"GOD SAVE THE QUEEN."**

MUSIC.
OVERTURE	... ...	BUSSONETTE.
CHORUS	... ... "Merry, Merry Cats are we."	THE CATS.
SONG	... ... "I've been to London Town." ...	DAME WIGGINS.
TRIO	... "We little Cats have lost our hats." JUMBO, KITTY and TOMMY.	
LULLABY & CHORUS	"Sleep gently, softly sleep." ...	TOMMY and CATS.
CHORUS	... ... "We little Cats all." ...	THE CATS.

6   *Dame Wiggins of Lee and her wonderful cats, 1889.*

Dame Wiggins of Lee
and her wonderful Cats
written and arranged for the Annual party at the Town Hall.
by Henry W Taunt - Oxford - Jan 2 & 3/89.

Opening—
Screen down, lime lights and Gas on – Instruments behind side wings – Cats take their places behind screen at the close of short overture – men ready with screen cords in hand –
Chorus opens behind, after the middle of 1st verse the curtain rises, and Cats come forward singing
At the last Miaw of 3rd verse Dame Wiggins comes on and Cats crowd round her still singing –

Chorus of Cats –   Merry merry Cats are we –

Merry merry Cats are we are we
Merry merry Cats are we
No blyther Cats there cannot be
Than those of Dame Wiggins of Lee
Miaw! Miaw! Miaw! Miaw! Miaw! Miaw! Miaw!
We belong to Dame Wiggins of Lee –

Merry Merry Cats are we are we
Merry merry Cats are we
No grief or Care have we to share
We Cats of Dame Wiggins of Lee
Miaw! Miaw! Miaw! &c –
We all love Dame Wiggins of Lee –

The Cats Chorus

Mer-ry Mer-ry Cats are we, are we – Mer-ry Mer-ry cats are we

No bly-ther Cats there cannot be – Than those of Dame Wiggins of Lee

Miau Miau Miau Miau Miau Mi-aw Mi-au –

We belong to Dame Wiggins of Lee –

7   9–10 Broad Street, *c.* 1890

As Taunt's business increased, his small shop in Cornmarket became more and more inadequate, and in 1874 he leased 9 and 10 Broad Street, spending ' as much as £1,000 in raising the whole building two storeys, adding four rooms and a gallery, extending the shop, and adding in other ways to the value of the property '.[7] A catalogue issued at this time shows that he and his assistants had taken over 3,000 photographs which could be purchased in 5 different series at prices ranging from 6d to 3/6 each. In addition, they were always ready to photograph ' Gentlemen's Seats, Churches, Interiors, Groups &c', whatever the distance involved. In their new premises, which were ' fitted with every appliance for producing the finest artistic work ', Taunt & Co. had every reason ' to thank their friends and the public for the increasing favours they had received '.

The cost of moving into Broad Street and his competitive prices forced Taunt to look for other ways of increasing his income. In 1874, he established a picture-framing manufactory in Boxall's Yard behind his Broad Street premises. Four years later, he was advertising a cycle shop in New Inn Hall Street where all leading makes of bicycles and tricycles were obtainable, and ' where gentlemen passing through Oxford can leave their Machines and have them put straight '. He also offered to provide information about the roads around Oxford, relying upon his knowledge as a keen cyclist whose photographic expeditions were often made by bicycle.

Much more important for the future was Taunt's decision to expand his publishing activities, and, eventually, to do his own printing. *A New Map of the River Thames* had been Taunt's first publication in 1872, while he was still at 33 Cornmarket Street. His shop in Broad Street offered more facilities for this work, however, and later editions of his book on the Thames, as well as catalogues and a guide to Hughenden, were published there in the later 1870s and 1880s. During these years, Taunt became interested in printing his own books, but lack of space posed problems, and he concentrated upon building up what has been described as ' a collection of some of the finest types ever designed in the Victorian period '. At last, in 1889, he leased Canterbury House in Cowley Road, and established a photographic and printing works in its extensive grounds.[8]

He re-named the house *Rivera* as a tribute to his beloved River Thames, and, after closing his branch at High Wycombe, he installed Miss Miles there as his tenant.

The decision to concentrate all his activities in Oxford may have had sound financial motives, but Taunt always ploughed most of his profits back into the business, and still had very little capital when the lease of 9–10 Broad Street expired at the end of 1894. According to him, the lessor—Alderman Carr—had promised to renew the lease after twenty-one years if improvements had been made to the property. This obligation had been fulfilled twenty years earlier, but Carr's executors were unconvinced, locked Taunt out of the shop, held its fittings as security and demanded £225 plus costs and a year's rent. With bad debts amounting to over £1,300 (Taunt put the figure at £3,200), liabilities of £1,118 and assets of only £999 7s. 5d, Taunt could only reply by filing a bankruptcy petition. It was a harrowing time, and he later wrote: 'I had lost everything, and nearly myself, except honour and my "Little Lady"'—his pet name for Fanny Miles. He was much indebted to her for both moral and financial support, and thanked her in a touching poem, entitled *Sweet Violets Grow Under the Snow*:

> ' Oh! troubles were great, my friends seem'd all fled,
> All but one, who closer did grow.
> To her do I owe the fact that I lived,
> Through my terrible blizzard and snow.'

As soon as he had been discharged, Taunt came to an agreement with Carr's executors by which he took the Broad Street fittings. He claimed to have lost nearly £400 by having to leave his old premises, but his business scarcely seems to have suffered, and he had moved to 41—later 34—High Street by 16 February 1895.

8 *Rivera* from Cowley Road, *c.* 1910.

9 Taunt and a lady—probably Fanny Miles—on his houseboat, c. 1890.

10 Randolph Adams and his first wife, c. 1890.

After the bankruptcy, Taunt gradually retreated into the background as far as taking photographs was concerned. He continued to make annual expeditions down the Thames in a much more luxurious boat,[9] and also went out by bicycle, but he was largely content to supervise the work of very capable assistants. The most important of these men was Randolph Adams, who had joined Taunt as a boy in 1885, and who became an expert in outdoor photography and darkroom work.[10] In these years, Adams would pedal a heavy quadricycle laden with equipment while Taunt sat in the front seat and indicated the scenes to be photographed. There were other photographers on Taunt's staff before the 1914–18 war—Harry Lord was one—but Adams was his personal assistant, and took most of the later Taunt photographs. Only Blenheim Palace remained the exclusive preserve of Taunt himself, both because it offered unique artistic opportunities and, according to rumour, because Taunt had designs on the Duke's housekeeper, Mrs. Crockett.

If Taunt's interest, or at least his involvement, in photography was decreasing, he was far from idle, and became well-known for the books which he published between 1900 and 1914. Before 1900, Taunt's reputation as author and publisher rested mainly upon his highly successful guides to the Thames which the *New York Times* had thought to be ' as essential as the boat for a successful journey '. In subsequent years, however, a constant stream of guide books began to appear, enabling the tourist ' to easily visit the places presented to your notice, and quickly grasp the most interesting points in connection with them '. These guides covered not only Oxford and district, but also places as far afield as Netley Abbey in Hampshire, condensing 'all the information which could be collected from every reliable source into as concise a form as possible'. *Country Life* described *Abingdon Ancient and Modern* as ' a careful, chatty and well illustrated book ', and this comment could equally have been applied to Taunt's other books. The extent of his caution is best revealed in *The Rollright Stones*, where Taunt listed the various theories about their origin, and stated that the correct answer ' was most possibly to be found in a combination of several, or even in the whole of them '. Occasionally, this caution might be thrown to the winds, but his books generally achieved what they set out to do, and show him to have been a useful historian as well as an excellent photographer.

Although he was producing guide books at a remarkable speed—no less than seven being written, printed and published in 1909—Taunt still had time for other activities, and, in 1908, began to edit an irregular newspaper, *Notes and News From Oxford's Famous City*. To some extent, this paper expressed Taunt's opinions on local and national affairs, but it also advertised the new lines which he was introducing. In 1908, for instance, he offered ' Christmas and Greeting cards with original views and scenes, and a number of pretty presents for Xmas and the New Year, in the way of Calendars, Plush Goods &c, &c, with Oxford and other Scenes upon them '. Six years later, he was encouraging firms to have their business circulars printed by Taunt & Co., where ' they mix their work with brains, and turn out work worth looking at a second time '.

Despite this diversification, the early 1900s were not without problems, and the onset of cheap picture postcards drastically reduced the sale of souvenir photographs, forcing Taunt to produce his own series of postcards.[11] At first, these were just black and white reproductions of his own photographs, but he went on to publish postcards with ornate surrounds, and, finally, attractive Aquarelle, or tinted, postcards printed from tone blocks. These last ' added to the monochrome photograph the harmonious colouring found in nature ', and at 6 for 6½d, sought to compete in price with the ' crude gaudiness of the common German post cards, which are often a hideous combination of the brightest colours thrown together in the worst possible taste '.

The variety of products being offered by Taunt & Co., and its well-established position as a photographic firm, probably led Taunt to give up his High Street premises in 1906, and operate solely from *Rivera*.[12] Even if he still

May Day Festivities. May Garlands, Oxford. Taunt & Co. 1194

11   A Taunt postcard, *c.* 1905.

12   The Printing and photographic works, *Rivera*, 1903.

encouraged people to visit his Cowley Road works, Taunt no longer needed to rely upon casual custom, and the bulk of his orders must have come from personal requests, and from the travellers who journeyed around Southern England showing samples to his agents in many towns and villages. In the years before 1914, Taunt had about twelve employees, and the works at *Rivera* included a large handicraft room, a printing works and storage space for thousands of glass negatives.[13]

The outbreak of war brought an end to the Indian Summer of Taunt & Co., but the true decline of the business was longer delayed. His staff was at once reduced to a minimum, and many economies had to be made, but he had an invaluable helper in Adams, who worked tirelessly, taking and developing photographs, printing and even distributing material himself. As a result, the photographic business continued, and Taunt was also able to produce such items as war-time greeting cards, calendars, and patriotic songs. In 1918,

however, Adams was called up for war-work, and Taunt described his absence as 'a paralysing loss now [that] I am seventy-six . . . What we shall do without him, I don't know . . . and we have no one to replace him, as we gave everybody to the country at the beginning of the war as Englishmen should'. Although he returned the following year, the business never regained its old momentum, and, when Taunt died at *Rivera* on 4 November 1922, it consisted only of Adams, his son William, and three girls.

When friends were quoted as saying that 'Taunt . . . has always some new idea in hand, and a heap of these are well worth consideration', they were unconsciously summarising his career. Mere success had never been enough; he had always to be doing something better than before, or turning his attention to new problems. He had built up his business by a mixture of hard work and inherent ability, and it never entered his head to take life more easily. He would probably have been less happy if he had.

13 Handicraft Room at *Rivera*, c. 1910.

3. HIS CHARACTER AND PERSONALITY

He could talk to you like a father, he could be a real dear old chap—and he could play merry blazes.

W. Adams, son of Randolph Adams, 7 January 1972

Taunt's career, with photography the only continuous thread in a tangled skein of other activities, reveals, to some extent, the complexity of the man. That he was clever and highly talented nobody denied, but although some were attracted by his strong and forthright personality, others were annoyed, and even scandalised, by it.

Memories of Taunt's appearance, and especially his height, have become distorted over the years, but photographs show him to have been a tall, distinguished man with a full beard. Few forgot this beard, or the nautical garb of reefer jacket and yachting cap which made Taunt so distinctive a figure along the Thames and elsewhere.[14] He was also well-known by the children of East Oxford, who would warn each other of his approach by saying ' look out, here comes old Skelly Taunt '.

Taunt's range of interests was at least as impressive as his appearance, and was indeed remarkable in a man who was largely self-educated. His knowledge of history and architecture, for example, is revealed both in his books, and in lectures such as the one on *The Lost and Destroyed Churches of Oxford* which he gave at the Ashmolean Museum on 1 March 1916. He realised the importance of maps to the local historian at a time when this was quite unusual, remarking that they ' often tell the story of a place in a way which is more true and forcible than any other '. His writings were enlivened by personal observations—one of the most evocative being his impression of Chipping Norton market-place with people shopping, ' a Salvation Army band murdering the music of a lively tune ', and a small group gathered round a Socialist speaker, listening ' listlessly . . . as if [it was] no concern of theirs '. Although Taunt's works were never intended to be academic, they are not without interest, and his historical leanings encouraged him to photograph scenes, streets and buildings which might otherwise have been forgotten.

Taunt was also fascinated by the more social side of history, and obviously enjoyed studying how people had lived in previous generations. He wrote about May Day customs in Oxford and Iffley, and published a small booklet on the history of St. Giles' Fair in 1907. In addition, he looked at the origins of historical relics like the court of the Slovens, or Sclavonians, in Oxford, which, amidst much drinking, had tried and soaked non-freemen found in the Town Hall Yard during civic elections. Symbolic of this interest in social history was Taunt's membership of the Ancient Order of Druids, which had been founded to collect

14 By Wallingford Bridge, *c.* 1870. Probably the earliest surviving photograph of Taunt.

information about the original Druids, and to uphold their principles of Justice, Philanthropy and Brotherhood. Taunt was an important figure in the Albion Lodge at Oxford—being a one-time Noble Arch-Druid, and he wrote its centenary souvenir in 1912.

An amateur botanist, Taunt was clearly well-informed about wild flowers. Linda Herring recalled meeting him on Cowley Marsh, and being shown *viper's bugloss, bladder campion* and *birds foot trefoil*. To his great delight, she repeated the names when next they met. Taunt's enjoyment of botany was very real and sympathetic, for he would admire and photograph plants, but warned potential pickers: ' be tender with these lovely flowers: if you gather one or two well and good, but do not tear up every blossom you can find, leaving none to seed '.

Music was another of Taunt's life-time interests, serving partly as a hobby and also as an aid to his business. He was a good pianist and organist, having an American pipe organ at *Rivera,* and—much earlier—acting as organist and choir leader in St. Mary Magdalene church. He was also a member of the Oxford Philharmonic and Choral Societies which put on quarterly choral concerts. This background as a singer and performer proved invaluable to Taunt when it came to planning his entertainments, and he became a successful composer of comic songs. In more serious vein, he produced a revised version of the National Anthem in 1901, and, during the First World War, a song entitled *Every Man a Soldier* which—to his delight—was approved by Field Marshal Lord Roberts.

Taunt's poems, or ' jingles ' as he preferred to call them, played a similar role; some were merely for the amusement of himself and his friends, others were for sentimental or commercial purposes. In the first category, one could include poems like:

IOU Ten pounds two
Received today, I will repay—
Many thanks, just what I want,
Truly yours, Henry Taunt.

or

We live in the wilds of Cowley Road,
And after our day's work is done
We often want to go up into town,
To have our share of the fun.

Others were equally amusing, but were designed to publicise the services of Taunt & Co. For example, this gem from a calendar for 1916:

'Twill remind you every day,
Of friend Taunt's work, anyway,
And that he'll be pleased to hear,
From you any day this year.
Shall we send to him today?
Yes! please do, without delay.

In the same vein was a poem of 1914 which encouraged people to advertise in *Notes and News:*

The man who has a thing to sell
And goes and whispers down a well,
Is not so apt to cop the dollars
As he who climbs a tree and hollers.

A more satirical form of humour creeps into one of his jingles, directed as it was against the ' haves ' of North Oxford by a ' have not ' from the East[15]

OXFORD, from the Ordnance Survey.

The Map of Oxford forms an Ass,
　Much burdened with a heavy load,
And thus with all the rates to pass,
　The rider has a sharpen'd goad;
For this much smaller uppish class,
North Oxford, rides the Oxford Ass.

15　Taunt's opinion of North Oxford, *c.* 1900.

But some of Taunt's poems sound appallingly, even amusingly, sentimental to modern ears. A good example is his tribute to Fred Valters, who died while campaigning for the East Ward in 1908:

The Master saw best to call him away
From suffering dire from toil day by day.
This message came down from the Kingdom of Love,
There's a Seat for you here in the Council above.

One vote for Valters, a mark of respect,
Is what we are sure all would wish and respect.
Though down here below he was last on the roll,
He is call'd away home, the first on the Poll.

Similar sentiments also appear in his exquisite war-time greetings cards, reflecting attitudes which were common in England, but which can hardly have been shared by those in the trenches.[16]

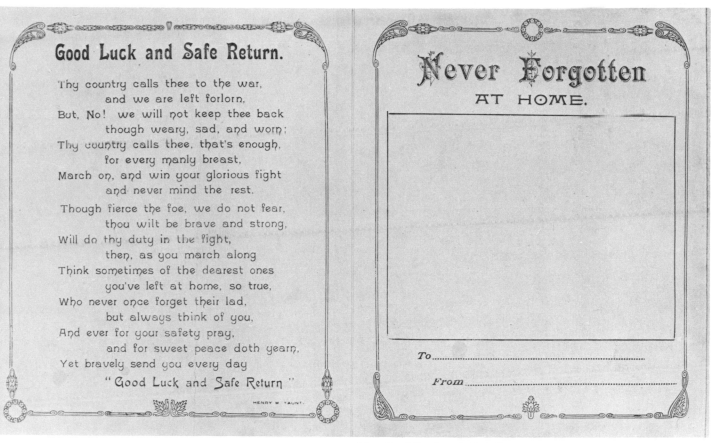

Good Luck and Safe Return.

Thy country calls thee to the war,
    and we are left forlorn,
But, No! we will not keep thee back
    though weary, sad, and worn;
Thy country calls thee, that's enough,
    for every manly breast,
March on, and win your glorious fight
    and never mind the rest.

Though fierce the foe, we do not fear,
    thou wilt be brave and strong,
Will do thy duty in the fight,
    then, as you march along
Think sometimes of the dearest ones
    you've left at home, so true,
Who never once forget their lad,
    but always think of you,
And ever for your safety pray,
    and for sweet peace doth yearn,
Yet bravely send you every day
    "Good Luck and Safe Return"

HENRY W TAUNT.

Never Forgotten
AT HOME.

To ....

From ....

16 *Good Luck and Safe Return, c.* 1915. The space is for a loved one's photograph— no doubt to be supplied by Taunt.

If some of Taunt's opinions appear, either directly or as indirectly, in his works and jingles, he was by no means averse to giving them a more public airing. Recalling his own origins, he was always sympathetic to the poor, giving a free Penny Reading in December 1875 'from his attachment to his fellow-parishioners', and, in 1880, noting sadly the destitution in St. Ebbe's. He bitterly opposed privilege, and attacked the government policies which caused unemployment, but he had no sympathy with Socialism, and claimed that ' the British working man has in many cases been so petted and humoured (even " peaceful picketing " is allowed him) that he has been led to believe himself above all law and order '.

A Conservative in national affairs, Taunt waged a constant war against party politics in local government, believing that they had nothing to do with ' carrying on our City Business, sweeping the streets, keeping up the roads, looking after the safety of people and their dwellings, collecting the Rates and spending the Rate-payers' money '. With this in mind, he stood as an Independent Candidate for the West Ward of the city in 1880, ' not as a nominee of any party, but purely as a business man and a Citizen '.[17] His independent status was, however, challenged, not only by the Liberal candidate, but also by his father, who very nearly stood against him. Taunt was defeated in that election after a spirited campaign, and again in 1881, when his address sought ' pure filtered cheap city water ', ' open and straightforward government ' and ' published accounts '. On both occasions, his support was far from minimal, but he seems to have kept out of municipal elections until 1906 and 1907, when he resolutely supported

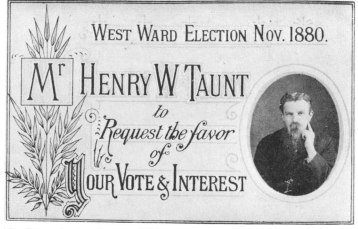

17 Taunt's election card, November 1880.

Valters, the Ratepayers' Association candidate for the East Ward. In 1908, he came close to contesting the Ward himself.[18] After complaining in vain for almost seven years, Taunt's anger was certainly justified, but he never carried out his threat to stand at the next election.

Taunt may only have made occasional attempts to reform the government of Oxford from within, but he was always a thorn in its flesh. As a rate-payer, he deplored any waste of public money, saving up most of his fury for a proposal by the Oxford Local Board to give the City Engineer, W. H. White, a bonus of £1,000 when the Main Drainage scheme was finished. On 10 March 1880, along with other petitioners, he wrote to the mayor, John Galpin, seeking to hire the

To the Burgesses of the East Ward

Ladies and Gentlemen,

The abominable and unhealthy practice is again being carried out, of putting Snow and Muck from the City, on the Children's Recreation Ground on the Cowley Road. Many of you know I have done what I can to stop this; which is harmful to the Children who play there, in every way. As my protests out of Council seem to be useless, I will ask you at the next opportunity to send me into the Council to fight the matter there, and look after the interests of the East Ward, as your present Aldermen and Councillors do not seem able to do this.

Faithfully Yours,

Henry W. Taunt

Rivera Cowley Road.
April 26, 1908.

18 Address to the Burgesses of the East Ward, 1908.

£180,000.!!
To Ratepayers of Oxford,

Brother Ratepayers,

Your Extravagant. and Reckless City Council, want to land you into spending at least £180,000., which will mean over that sum, besides an additional annual cost, all of which will have to come out of the rates.

They ask you to place yourselves entirely in their hands by allowing them to promote their Tramway Bill in Parliament, practically to "Open your mouths and shut your eyes and see what they'll put in."

"Its only Preliminary" they tell you, and afterwards when a failure, they will turn round and say, "You authorized us to do it."

JUDGE BY THE PAST.

The Drainage was to cost £48,000. It cost £203,000. The Town Hall was to cost £47,000., and not be a penny expence to the ratepayers. It cost £100,000., and is a big yearly expence. These are only two cases out of a number.

Our best policy is to WAIT ! If you pass this Tramway Bill you pledge yourselves without remedy afterwards, and then it will be PAY ! PAY ! PAY. !

Henry W. Taunt.

34, High Street, Oxford.

Printed and Published by the Rivera Press, Oxford.

19 Taunt against the Tramways Bill, 1905.

Town Hall for a protest meeting. Galpin twice put him off, trusting that ' you will treat my judgement with that courteous consideration which as Mayor and Chief Magistrate of the City I am certainly entitled to claim for at your hands '. Taunt, however, was ' unfortunately not at all impressed (well, except with the utter nonsense written) ', and arranged and spoke at a meeting in Gloucester Green which roundly condemned the Board's scheme. He later noted, with satisfaction, that the plan was abandoned in October 1880, although no account of this ever appeared in the local press.

As a self-appointed public watch-dog, Taunt was always quick to attack the local authority whenever controversial issues arose. From 1905, he mobilised opposition to the City Council's Tramways Bill, which sought to establish a municipal electric tram service, attacking it mainly on economic grounds.[19]

The Oxford Millenary celebrations of 1912 were another source of trouble, and his truculent tender for the right to photograph them was accompanied by a criticism of the Council for preparing to spend £250 of the ratepayers' money on a banquet for distinguished guests. One of his last actions was to produce a special edition of *Notes and News* in 1922 attacking the Council's plan to give the Town Clerk, Richard Bacon, a pension on his retirement.

If he was always ready to speak up on behalf of his fellow ratepayers, he was even more forthright about matters nearer home. After he had received a letter which presumably blamed his packaging for some damage in transit, Taunt's reply ended: ' please don't write childish twaddle but do your own business properly if you can, and wait until I ask you before you attempt to teach me how to manage mine '. Clearly, he was a man to reckon with, as the City found out when, in 1897, a high stile was placed at the entrance leading into the recreation ground opposite *Rivera*. Taunt at once wrote to the mayor, complaining that it prevented old people, ladies and young children from getting in, and that the top rail ' was utilized by young Roughs in the day time . . . and at night it is used for purposes which are usually done in dark corners '. Taunt's first two letters achieved nothing, and he wrote again on August 16, having worked out that nearly two hundred lads and children had sat on the stile during the previous Sunday: even worse, ' the night was made hideous by a girl and man at the stile—I need say nothing about the language used, which was, both in the evening, and at night, of the most debased character, revolting in every way '. No action was taken, however, and, on 11 April 1898, Taunt made one last appeal about the stile, threatening otherwise to write to the press, ' and if that does not do any good, *I shall quietly saw it down* '.

To judge from his letter about things 'usually done in dark corners', Taunt's morals would appear to have been beyond reproach, but they did, in fact, give rise to great controversy. In Septemter 1863, at the age of twenty-one, he married an Oxford dressmaker, Miriam Jeffrey, and the couple had two children, Roland and Cissie, whom Taunt came to dislike so much that he never mentioned them in his later writings. This in itself must have put a strain on the marriage, but Taunt also seems to have been fond of women in his early days, and, in about 1873, he met Fanny Miles, who was subsequently at his shop in High Wycombe. Rumour has it that there were illegitimate children from this relationship, but, if so, Taunt's mother set a strange seal upon it by going down to live with Miss Miles after Henry Taunt, senior, died in 1884. Fanny came back to Oxford in, or before, 1889, when she became tenant of *Rivera,* but Taunt and his wife may not have moved there until 1906. Subsequent arrangements at *Rivera* were almost bizarre with Mrs. Taunt—by now partially crippled—living in complete isolation upstairs, and Fanny acting as Taunt's companion and housekeeper. In view of her husband's long-standing attachment to Fanny, and his suspected affairs with other women, Mrs. Taunt might have been expected to begin divorce proceedings at some point, but she seems merely to have retired for several months at a time to live with her brother Edgar and his wife in Western Road. Although details concerning Taunt's private life are understandably sketchy, and sometimes conflicting, he does not appear in a favourable light, and some parents were even afraid to let their children go near him.

In some ways, Taunt was thus the archetypal Victorian, saying one thing and doing another, but this is no uncommon fault, and he had many compensating virtues. His talents, interests and sympathies speak for themselves, and, despite his anger, he was a tender-hearted man who preferred 'open hearted joyous fun at an unsophisticated picnic' to 'stiff garden parties and fetes'. He loved the countryside, its flowers and its animals, and his feelings for people are best summarised in his own words: 'We all think ourselves worst off; but if we only knew, we should find others worse [off] still.' To one child at least, he would always remain 'a dear old man . . . who looked like a cross between father Christmas and a very friendly gnome'[20].

20   Taunt with his horse and dog, *Rivera, c.* 1910.

4. TAUNT'S PHOTOGRAPHS

The photographer is a historian in himself—a historian who makes no mistakes, who has no prejudices, but who registers things just as he finds them.

Oxford Chronicle, discussing Taunt's work,
21 September 1911

Sixty-four years and over 53,000 negatives separated the first Taunt photograph of 1858 from the last—a view of a Ford lorry in Broad Street taken in August 1922. Those facts tell only part of the story, however, for his career as a photographer was remarkable not only because it was long and prolific, but also because his work was consistently excellent and reflected in full his many interests. This quality and scope have made his photographs as historically valuable today as they were commercially successful in his life-time.

Portrait and group photography always played an important part in a photographer's business, and Taunt soon became very adept at this work. He attained prominence in 1870, when his photograph of the Oxford Boat Race crew was praised for ' the uniform clearness of all the portraits '. In the following year, more publicity resulted from a successful High Court action in which Taunt sued Theresa Conroy, a London photographer, for pirating a picture of the Oxford crew, which he had registered under the title, ' Mr. Payne with his hat off '. Once his name was made, Taunt could rely upon a steady flow of private commissions, but he also photographed ordinary people wherever he went, showing them at work or relaxing in their own surroundings. By no means everyone was willing to pose for the camera, and Ben the fisherman openly ' feared them foot-hoggers ', feeling ' just as if I had been picked up and dabbed as flat as a pancake on a plate and stuck in a windy for ever '. Such anxieties about photography were also found in more elevated Oxford circles, and Benjamin Jowett, the Master of Balliol, refused to let Taunt take his photograph for many years. Such opposition was unusual, however, and, from the early days, large numbers of people were keen to have themselves, their families or their sporting achievements recorded by the celebrated Mr Taunt or his assistants.

Taunt's personal interests and business needs soon encouraged him to photograph street scenes, as well as historic and contemporary architecture. He built up a huge collection of negatives depicting not only Oxford and its surrounding towns and villages but also more distant places. Photographs of this kind were sold as souvenirs, published as postcards, or used to illustrate his many guide books. Some of them—for example, views of Magdalen College or Christ Church—must have sold in large numbers, but those which illustrated industrial or smaller domestic buildings can hardly have been in great demand, despite ' the sound judgement and artistic temperament ' which enabled Taunt to ' make such unpromising subjects as gasometers and waterworks look picturesque '. Such photographs were clearly intended for record purposes, and his collection preserves the appearance of many buildings and scenes which have now been destroyed, or completely altered by the trappings of modern society.

Taunt also excelled in landscape photography, and concentrated mainly upon the scenery of the river Thames and its tributaries. The early landscape photographer faced criticism on two fronts, for some regarded his work as inferior to that of the artist while others saw the photograph as a pale shadow of the real thing. In 1874, the *Evesham Journal* proved a harsh critic, but still had to admit that one of Taunt's photographs was ' more beautiful than the scene it represents '. From a less critical standpoint, *The Field* claimed that some of his Thames views ' rival in beauty the work of the most skilful draughtsman '. In landscape photography, as in other branches of the art, Taunt worked hard to achieve success, and spent more than thirty summers on the Thames, photographing all aspects of the river—its scenery, its people and its very character. In 1918, he declared that it had been ' a subject I have taken an interest in more than any other ', and his photographs bear out the truth of those words.

If pictures of people, architecture and landscape were most common, the total output of Taunt & Co. was much more varied. Quite apart from the demands of his customers, his own interests ensured that he photographed methods of transport, agricultural and industrial processes, social life and customs, wild flowers and, indeed, anything aesthetically beautiful. One group of photographs, for instance, shows the intricate patterns made by frost on a window pane— a sight now banished from centrally-heated homes.

After Taunt died, leaving everything to Miss Miles, the future of his photograph collection was uncertain. Miss Miles and her sister, Polly, continued to live at *Rivera* for some years, but the property was purchased by Frank Organ, the Oxford builder, who was faced by forbidding piles of postcards, manuscripts and papers, and by thousands of glass negatives. Many negatives were smashed up or cleaned off for use as greenhouse glass, but the local historian, Harry Paintin, realised what was happening, and contacted E. E. Skuce, the City Librarian, about buying the Taunt collection for the City Library. Mr. Skuce wasted no time in doing this, and, between 1924 and 1925, obtained several thousand negatives, as well as prints, papers and manuscript folders, at a cost of only £98 10s. 0d. Through the foresight of these two men, a unique collection of photographs was preserved for future generations to see, to learn from, or, simply, to admire. Taunt's death had removed ' a well-known figure from Oxford, but his numerous works ' were now certain to ' form a valuable and abiding memorial of his zeal and industry '.

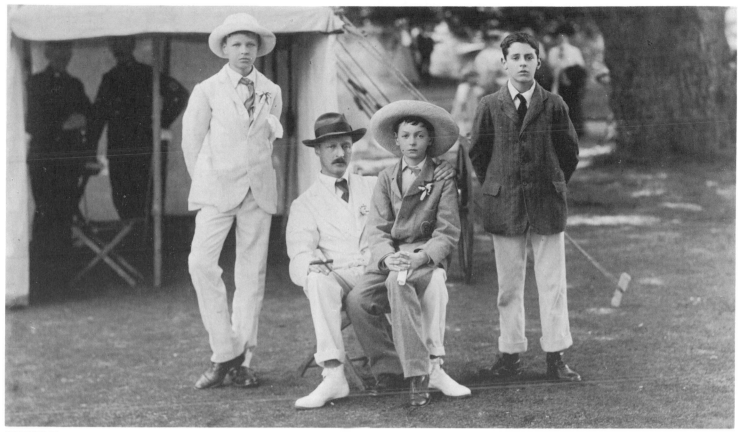

PEOPLE

Charles, 9th Duke of Marlborough and three boys, 1910. The Duke's casual elegance contrasts strongly with the shabby unease of the children.

The porter, Blenheim Palace, c. 1895. A daunting figure, secure in the knowledge that he was a Duke's servant.

(*Over*) Morrell's employees at Headington Hill Hall, c. 1903. This huge gathering had probably been invited to celebrate J. H. Morrell's 21st birthday.

Charles Robertson and his family, Apsley Paddox, Woodstock Road, 1913. A prosperous family group, with the son in fashionable sailor suit, and baby looking like an old advertisement for Sunlight soap.

Group at Henley Regatta, *c.* 1895. Some of the spectators, with picnic hampers and bottles of *Epernay* at the ready.

Ancient Order of Druids at Blenheim Palace, 11 August 1912. The serious figure standing in the centre of the group is Winston Churchill, who had just been initiated into the Order.

Blanket mill workers, Witney, *c.* 1895. Against a background of blankets, these men were probably posing before a camera for the first time.

Domestic servants training school, Headington Hill Hall, *c.* 1900. These girls were clearly destined to serve in the very best houses of the Oxford area.

A tinker and his customer, Moulsford, *c.* 1895. The itinerant tradesman was still a part of everyday life in the country; Taunt called this one ' Smock-frock,' and the girl ' Skirtie '.

Gipsy Smith, Henley, *c.* 1905. A familiar figure at Regattas for many years, she claimed that her ring had been the gift of a Duke.

James Lowe, lock keeper at Day's Lock, 1904. During his long association with the Thames, Taunt came to know and respect many of its characters. James Lowe was clearly one of them.

James Weller, sexton, Church Handborough, 1902. Taunt described him as ' having the stolid form and features of an honest, hard working English labourer '.

CUSTOMS AND AMUSEMENTS

Iffley on May Morning, 1906. The May-day procession round Iffley had formerly involved both old and young, but, by the turn of the century, only school children took part in it.

Hall's Oxford Brewery drays at the Plain, 1 May 1912. Now a forgotten part of Oxford's May Day celebrations, this procession was so long that Taunt had to combine two pictures to show it all.

Morris dancers outside the Chequers, Headington Quarry, 1898. Morris dancing was dying out in many places, but, in Headington Quarry, the tradition was preserved into this century.

St. Giles' Fair, 1895. Fairs were another traditional part of life, and thousands flocked to St. Giles' Fair in early September as they do today.

Burford Hiring Fair, *c.* 1890. The fair provided opportunities for amusement and gossip but hiring fairs were also occasions where working people and servants sought employment for the year ahead.

One-man band, Kelmscott, *c.* 1900. Few entertainments were provided, and the wandering musician could always be guaranteed an appreciative audience of children, and adults too.

Musicians with dancing monkey, Taplow, *c.* 1890. The one-man band is again employed, but a bizarrely-dressed monkey adds to the interest provided for the spectators.

Queen Victoria's Diamond Jubilee celebrations, Abingdon, 1897. Coronations and jubilees were great occasions, and, to some at least, the speeches were less exciting than the bands and processions.

Visit of the Prince and Princess of Wales, Wantage, 1897. Royal visits were another rare delight, attended and watched by hundreds, while bands played and bouquets were presented.

Skating on the Cherwell, 1895. Home-made amusements were most common, however, and a cold spell soon brought the adventurous onto the ice.

Children in the sheep-washing pool, Cowley, 1914. If ice is attractive in winter, how much more so is the sight and sound of water on a hot July day! These children were playing 'ducks and drakes' one month before the outbreak of the First World War.

Bank Holiday, Uffington Castle, 1899. Bank Holidays—introduced in 1871—brought new opportunities and new problems as large numbers of people hurried from towns and cities to beauty spots and seaside resorts. Pressure on the country-side had begun.

STREET SCENES

St. Aldate's, looking towards Carfax, 1907.   The tram-lines are very evident in a street of small shops and varied architecture; the City Librarian was already complaining about traffic noise.

Magdalen College Tower from the West, 1907.   This famous tower, built between 1492 and 1509, has now lost the frame of lime trees that paid so fine a compliment to its man-made beauty.

Cornmarket Street, 1902.   A busy scene photographed while Oxford was celebrating the coronation of Edward VII.

High Street, looking west from The Queen's College, c. 1887.   The majestic sweep of the High, leading the eye past the famous sycamore tree to the 14th Century spire of St. Mary's Church.

Broad Street, *c.* 1875. Once known as Horsemonger Street, Broad Street was where Oxford's horse fairs took place. Today, its width is usually masked by parked cars.

Castle Street and New Road junction, *c.* 1888. While a man re-lays cobbles, children are gathering round a Punch and Judy Show. This attractive area, known more recently as Macfisheries Corner, has now disappeared under the Westgate Centre.

(*Over*) Market Place, Witney, 1900. Another peaceful scene with the Marlborough Hotel bus awaiting customers, and a small boy watching events from his position by the lamp post.

Upper Fisher Row, *c.* 1885. A group of the 17th Century cottages pulled down before 1900. These houses had some pleasing features—their prominent dormer windows for example—but they were in a very poor condition.

Hollybush Row, 1906. St. Thomas's was a poor, but lively, district of Oxford, where squalor co-existed with the picturesque. Unfortunately, in erasing one we have also lost the other.

Lake Street, New Hinksey, *c.* 1895. The low-lying suburbs of Oxford were often flooded, and their Venetian appearance drew large crowds of sightseers. In this case, the name of the street became singularly appropriate.

Sheep Street, Bicester, *c.* 1895. In country towns, the roads were normally quiet, and people kept off them because of the dirt, not the danger.

Hart Street, Henley, *c.* 1890. Wide and empty streets came to life on market days, and parking could become a problem.

Crowmarsh Gifford, *c.* 1892. Village streets were almost deserted for large parts of the day, and dust blew from their unmetalled surfaces during dry weather.

Littlemore, *c.* 1902. In winter, country roads became rutted and muddy, and pedestrians could find them difficult to cross.

ARCHITECTURE

Catte Street, looking south past the Bodleian Library, 1904. The superb juxtaposition of cube, cylinder and cone remarked upon by Thomas Sharp in *Oxford Observed*.

Christ Church from St. Aldates, *c.* 1890.   Defiantly sited below the brow of a hill, Wren's noble Tom Tower (1681–82)
provides a perfect foil for the 16th Century facade of Christ Church.

Brasenose College, Radcliffe Square front, *c.* 1885. Except for the railings around the Radcliffe Camera, which were removed in 1936, the view is unchanged today.

Trinity College Chapel, *c.* 1880. Bathurst's chapel (1691–94) before the President's Lodgings of 1885–87 were built to the east of it.

New College, 1901. A glimpse of Basil Champney's Robinson Tower through a gate in the old city wall.

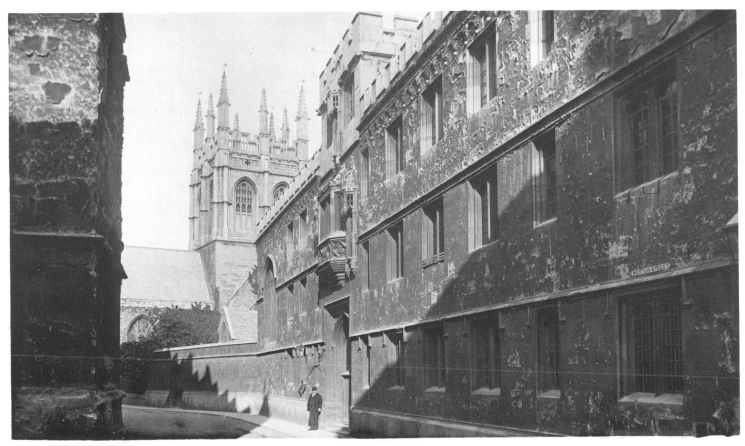

Merton Street, looking East, *c.* 1890. The angle of the sun leads the eye across the front of Corpus Christi College towards the chapel of Merton College.

The University Museum, from South Parks Road, *c.* 1885.   This view was blocked for ever by the building of the Radcliffe Science Library, but it showed Deane and Woodward's design to best advantage.   The Museum was built between 1855 and 1860.

Laud's Library, St. John's College, 1916.   Supplementing the old library of 1598, this one was built at Archbishop Laud's expense between 1631 and 1633.

Magdalen College, stone figures in the cloister, c. 1880. Looking as though they have been discovered plotting in a corner, these figures seem surprised and hostile.

Blenheim Palace, first State Room, 1900. This room, with its beautiful furnishings and Gobelin tapestries, is seen by thousands of people every year. The portrait of Consuelo, wife of the 9th Duke of Marlborough, still hangs above the fireplace.

St. Giles' church from the South-East, c. 1892. Like most churches, St. Giles' church contains the work of many generations. The early 13th Century Transitional windows of the tower stand out beyond the South chapel, which was largely rebuilt in about 1850.

Christ Church Cathedral Choir, *c.* 1900. The magnificent 15th Century lierne vaulting is depicted with remarkable clarity in this view.

Burford church, interior, looking East, 1901. Two old roof lines and a blocked 12th Century window are clearly visible on the East wall of the nave, which attained its present form in the 15th Century.

High Street, Burford, 1901. The children standing outside it add to the charm of this 16th Century house with its three gables and oriel windows.

White Hart Hotel, Cornmarket Street, 1901. This timber-framed, 17th Century house had been altered by the insertion of sash windows and a Victorian ground floor. It was demolished and replaced by 'a first-class hotel restaurant' in 1901.

High Street, Banbury, *c.* 1875. A wealthy merchant's house of 1650, showing richly ornamented timber-framing and decorative plasterwork.

George Hotel, Dorchester, *c.* 1900. The yard of this old coaching inn was given over to hens and small boys during the Railway Age.

Little Stoke, *c.* 1895. A labourer's cottage, crudely extended, this house seems to have grown out of the very earth.

RIVER THAMES

Moulsford Reach, *c.* 1885. This beautiful photograph taken in winter sunshine instantly captures Taunt's love for the Thames.

Whitchurch in winter, *c.* 1885. Another view chosen with infinite care and great artistic sensitivity.

Eynsham Old Weir, *c.* 1880.   When Taunt first knew the Thames, its upper reaches still contained many hazards like this primitive weir.   The rough pole swung back to allow boats to pass.

Iffley Lock, *c.* 1885.   In the later 19th Century, there was a campaign to remove this lock because it held back the Thames, and increased the danger of flooding in Oxford.   Owing to a lack of money, it survived until 1924.

Bablockhythe Ferry, c. 1880. Most ferries have now disappeared, but they were an intrinsic part of the old river, dating back many centuries.

Rebuilding Day's Lock Weir, 1885. In the last decades of the 19th Century, many improvements were carried out, and navigation was made much safer for the increasing number of pleasure boats.

Camping out at Hart's Wood, 1880. Camping parties became common, and this one was clearly determined to enjoy all the creature comforts.

The river at Oxford during Eights week, *c.* 1905. One of Oxford's great sporting and social events, Eights Week attracted huge crowds onto the river and its towpath.

Colonel Goode's boat, *Coronation*, Sutton Courtenay, 1911. The wealthy took to their own boats, using their riverside homes as a base for expeditions on the river.

Sandford Paper Mill and the *King's Arms*, 1904. The river was not only a place of recreation, but industry and enjoyment could co-exist quite happily.

Launching a lifeboat from Salter's Yard, Folly Bridge, *c.* 1900. Boat-building was a small but important industry in Oxford, and boats from Salter Brothers were exported to the Congo, India and China.

TRANSPORT

Floods on the Great Western Railway near North Hinksey, 1875. Railways were so much a part of everyday life that Taunt rarely photographed them. On this occasion, flooding made the scene memorable.

London and North Western Railway Station, Park End Street, 1914. Opened in 1852, this station is supposed to contain surplus ironwork from the previous year's Great Exhibition. Ironically, it is now a tyre depot.

Swinford toll bridge, near Eynsham, *c.* 1885. Once a common sight, the toll-gate is now rare, but drivers still have to pay to cross Swinford Bridge.

The Burford Bus outside The Bull Hotel, Burford, *c.* 1890. Burford was poorly served by railways, and road passenger transport continued to be well-patronised.

Trams in the High Street, *c.* 1890. Oxford's horse trams operated from 1881 until 1914, when they were superseded by motor buses.

The Ancient Order of Foresters' outing at the Greyhound Inn, Besselsleigh, 1908. In addition to ordinary public services, horse brakes, and later charabancs, were available for group outings.

Banbury market place, c. 1880. Carriers played an important part in transport, taking goods and people to market and linking scattered communities together.

Despatching blankets from Early's blanket mill, Witney, *c.* 1895. Local road hauliers, like W. Payne & Son, could even profit from railway goods traffic by becoming agents to the local railway company.

Streatley Mill from the Bridge, *c.* 1897. The presence of the barge, *Cicero*, shows that the Thames was still being used for the carriage of goods, but this traffic was on a much smaller scale than it had been.

Wantage from the Berks and Wilts Canal basin, *c.* 1895. The water-lilies and the dilapidated narrow boat, *Madeline,* reveal the general decline of canals in the later 19th Century. For fishing, however, they remained ideal.

Chauffeur-driven car at Apsley Paddox, Woodstock Road, 1913. The car, though still for the wealthy, was becoming much more common. Few realised how dominant it would become.

AGRICULTURE
Fulbrook Farm, 1906. The substantial stone buildings are of a time when the most important changes in agriculture were seasonal ones.

Horse ploughing, *c.* 1900. Two teams wait patiently before driving another straight furrow up the field.

Threshing, Great Rissington, *c.* 1895. A labourer using the flail to separate the wheat from the chaff.

Reaping, *c.* 1900. To a large extent, harvesting was still done by hand, but this horse-drawn reaper was the fore-runner of increasing mechanisation.

Potato planting, *c*. 1900.   Victorian inventiveness is typified by this adaptation of the wheelbarrow to the planting of seed potatoes.

A shepherd with his flock, Cowley Road, *c*. 1900.   An age-old scene, but with the difference that Taunt's house stands in the background.   This area is now completely built-up, and *Rivera* stands next to the bus garage.

Sheep washing, Radcot Bridge, *c.* 1890.   To rid them of insect pests, the sheep were tossed into the river and thoroughly immersed before being allowed to climb back on to dry land.

Sheep shearing, *c.* 1895.   Using traditional hand-shears, four men make short work of removing the wool, while a fifth gathers the fleeces together.

Catching moles, *c.* 1890. Armed with sticks and a trap, the mole catcher sets about an unpleasant task now more often undertaken by zealous gardeners.

Jersey cattle and milkmaids, Headington Hill Hall, 1917. An idyllic scene far removed from the hygienic world of milking machines and pasteurisation.

Horse fair, Bampton, 1904. The centre of agricultural life with farmers and labourers coming in to buy and sell, or just to look and talk.

Sheep fair, Thame, 1897. Another gathering of the farming community, with a sale in progress outside the Nag's Head.

Going home from Bampton Fair, 1904.   Farmers well satisfied with their purchases had time to quench their thirsts at the Chequers in Brize Norton.

Windmill, Great Milton, 1901.   The traditional routine was beginning to break down, however, and steam power had left this fine post-mill derelict and unused.

CRAFTS AND INDUSTRY

Blacksmith at work, *c.* 1895. The blacksmith was at the heart of the village community, not only shoeing horses but also making and repairing agricultural implements.

S. W. Smith, Wheelwright's shop, Kidlington, *c.* 1905. The wheelwright was as versatile a craftsman as the blacksmith, and could turn his hand to all forms of carpentry.

Brickfield, Culham, *c*. 1880. A small brickfield with its own kiln, conveniently situated so that the bricks could be transported by water.

Castle Mills, Paradise Street, Oxford, 1901. There was probably a mill on this site in 1086, and the city's corn was ground here for centuries. The mill was demolished in 1929.

Church Army Press, Temple Road, Cowley, *c.* 1910. This small printing works was established in a disused Congregational chapel early in this Century.

Swan Brewery, Oxford, 1907. Brewing in Oxford was established by the 13th Century, and Morrell's still carry on the tradition. The Swan Brewery, formerly part of Hall's Oxford Brewery Ltd., was where Telephone House now stands.

Steamroller, Oxfordshire Steam Ploughing Company, Cowley, *c.* 1905. Now known as John Allen & Sons (Oxford)
Ltd., this firm was founded in 1868, and has specialised in making agricultural machinery and steamrollers.

Cooper's Oxford Marmalade factory, Park End Street, Oxford, *c.* 1910. The women are preparing the oranges for the
next stage of Frank Cooper's secret recipe. Cooper opened a shop in the High Street before 1840, and began making
marmalade in the 1870s.

(*Over*) Widening Magdalen Bridge, 1883. The 18th Century bridge was widened by twenty feet on the south side, but the
original design was faithfully copied.

SOURCES

Early life

Census of England and Wales, 1841, Oxford, St. Ebbe's

H. W. Taunt, *Kirtlington, Oxon*, [1905]; *Reminiscences of 50 years Ago*, 1913; *Old St. Ebbes*, 1912; *Festival of Winter;* *Cumnor Hill; Jingles Volume* 3 (unpublished books)

Oxford Times, 26 May 1913

Oxford Chronicle, 10 November 1922

Oxford Journal Illustrated, 8 November 1922

Oxford Chronicle, 10 November 1922

Career

Register of Electors for the City of Oxford, 1866

Oxford City Directories, 1871–2, 1874, 1878

Valter's Oxford and District Postal Directory, 1895–6

H. W. Taunt, *Fairford Church, with its celebrated windows* [1905]; *Princes Risborough and Round It* [1910]; *The Rollright Stones* [1907]; *Catalogue of Henry W. Taunt & Co.'s Views* [1874]; *Notes and News,* nos. 6, 9 and 13; *Reminiscences of 50 years Ago,* 1913; *Up the Thames in the Christmas Holidays;* *Jingles Volume 3; Shiplake* (unpublished books)

Newspaper cuttings Books 1868–78; 1874–1907

Letter to M. Adams, 15 July 1918

Jacksons Oxford Journal, 11 March 1871

Oxford Times, 9 February—4 May 1895

Oxford Journal Illustrated, 8 November 1922

Information: W. Adams, son of Randolph Adams
            Sir Basil Blackwell

The Man

City Letters 1897–8

H. W. Taunt, *Kirtlington, Oxon* [1905]; *Official souvenir of the centenary of the Albion Lodge, Oxford,* 1912; *Down the River to Nuneham and Abingdon* [c. 1905]; *Reminiscences of 50 years ago,* 1913; *History of the Slovens or Sclavonians;* *Holywell; Jingles; Maps and Plans* (unpublished books)

Newspaper Cuttings Books, 1868–76, 1874–1907

Notes and News, nos. 5, 6, 11 and 13

Manifesto on behalf of F. Valters, 1907

Information: W. Adams.
            W. Cordrey.
            Mrs. Linda Herring.
            Mrs. E. P. Musto, Taunt's niece.
            Miss K. M. Nichols.

The photographs

Oxford City Council Library Committee minutes, 1913–27

H. W. Taunt, *New Map of the River Thames* [1872]; *The Master, Benjamin Jowett* (unpublished book)

Newspaper Cuttings Book, 1868–78

Letter to A. Preston, March 1918

Jackson's Oxford Journal, 15 April 1871

THE PROPOSED DESECRATION OF OXFORD.

CAUTION!!

TO EVERY LOVER OF OUR BEAUTIFUL CITY.

The Tramway Co. are proposing to destroy the beauty of our principal Streets by erecting POSTS and carrying OVERHEAD WIRES along them, and although this is known among the City Councillors, the word has evidently been passed to 'say nothing' until the Municipal Elections are over, so that you should not have the chance of voting against it.

The beauty of Oxford is one of its greatest charms, and is a valuable source of revenue to the City and its traders, which Posts and overhead Wires would decididly damage, as they have done in other towns; this every lover of our City should do their utmost to prevent.

This very idea has already been condemned; to allow it would be to desecrate Oxford, but it can be prevented by your refusing to vote for any Candidate who will not pledge himself to oppose it both in and out of the City Council, and vote only for those who will pledge themselves to do this. The matter is all important, it is not a party question in any way, but the very fact of its being kept back until after the elections plainly shows that you are not to have a voice in deciding against it.

Imagine our High Street, "The Glory of Oxford," with a double line of posts stretching across and overhead wires running up; and do not allow such a vandalism to be carried out, but oppose it now. Next year is the Millenium of our History, shall it be remembered by the desecration of our charming streets?

Yours faithfully,

Henry W. Taunt

Rivera, Cowley Road.
October 21st. 1911.